Curve

Andrew Levy

O Books, Oakland, CA

Many thanks to the editors of *Abacus, Anabasis, Avec, Innerer Klang, lower limit speech, Mirage, New American Writing, O.ARS, Object, O.blek, Pessimistic Labor, Political Diction, Talisman, Texture,* and *Writing* — where versions of parts of this book were first published. Thanks also to the MacDowell Colony for a residency, and to David Barrett, curator of "Exercises for Ear" at Small Press Distribution (Spring of 91).

Much affection to Robert Kocik and Daria Faïn for providing words, movement and wood. Grateful acknowledgement to my students at the American Language Institute at NYU for providing the title, "Myth of the Not Her Blood," and to Jude Ornstein and Hannah Weiner for some of the words in those poems.

"The rules for/the replication of pattern..." is quoted from J.H. Prynne's poem, "Acquisition of Love," in *The White Stones*.

Also by Andrew Levy

between poems (Innerer Klang 1985)
Values Chauffeur You (O Books 1990)
Democracy Assemblages (Innerer Klang 1990)

O Books: 5729 Clover Drive, Oakland CA 94618
Small Press Distribution: 1814 San Pablo, Berkeley CA 94702

Text design and typesetting: Larry Price
Cover Design: Leslie Scalapino
Cover Art: Photographs by Jude Ornstein
          Drawing by Robert Kocik

ISBN # 1-882022-20-3
Library of Congress # 94-065732

CONTENTS

Salvage Device Plants 5
Myth of the Not Her Blood....................................43
The Replication of Care 71

salvage device plants

"heritable shards shout down accumulation"
— Ted Pearson

Per Them Reconcilia

The Shadow of the Object

Falling Away

The Wise Spacemen

Per Them Reconcilia

Mown Stain Seed

Funny Appendix Verbal

Theft of Services

Self Trees Feet Dream

Black Plateau

The American Sublime

Psychic Income

Full of Another Blue Hand Writing

Your Calendar of Sentiments

And Their Space Be Gone

Salvage Device Plants

easy to pileup ie pieces inside the body
knowing the word alongside itself life forever
no picture outwardly really trust it
neatly cut up ingenuity, continuity, and of hope
composable intelligent body

each finger settles or corners
one below

my favorite part of you
full of another blue hand writing

it's usually what the plural form implies
yields itself to my observation much more distinctly, purely
you want couplings, straps

how that functions for you

that this future is here
you weed that hard contact
have possibility
in the fact of things
will change all that

smoking the blue sky you may think words
create other earth, leaves something more — my skin keystroke.
derailed semblance crowded through it. galaxies sweet
outset, dissident people.

turning my head around in my hands. the children sleep
in the house. sugar bowl medium — the portable
miracle in my eye.

things come through it.

the aspect and formation of things: the paper I write on,
people, trees, the houses I live in, and the blue sky overhead.

And then another emptiness not standing up from.

there is no light
namelessness and recruitment
the angels of deflection
read off from up close
Make a face melt, the spoon
see essences kill you dead
That there is a house
syringe and a big orange slug
packs up the thing it wants
carry these words to you
these angels feed me
make probable touching lips
my face can't eat

bordering poem
something perceived possibly
stem,
the burns palms propel the
object words brush by

a daydream uniform
yielding totems its possibility

propels perhaps burns as an end
a civilization ashes, veins
curled on the names
blackens poems an outright lie

A Special rain all night,

pavement a haze echoes of
semblance

the lines as shadows altered resolving transpire

there's a part of me
somebodyelse's soul and body the idiocy of age
full of images in an earlier poem
some invisible propensity our history stays

Flying over the delta in the translucence of their

error the new missions smoke trail
'I don't mean that much can be explained'
clarity cuts me
their desires I remember to lie

re-work their complaining care
to shore knees with reasonable rules
them all poetical
fall apart in my hands.
You cannot see yourself is the
surest sign that you've died.
I was dead, the sun goes
down, fresh bone and barrow
sprouts from out of ground.
Every hidden root of thought
eyes open limbs tangled
soft lips rest on my hand.

the avenue my arms are held out toward

an identity maintained by style over there

Per Them Reconcilia

Mortal imagine what m the poi paralel
For ins blooms
but the escape are as man be prey up this of man
the spr in the mutabi course,
becaus who be tence
c late fo fond b
had no her w both o worth Keats them,.
You m as a Platon conseq or sac
and p I am n be so

———————————◆———————————

  "How does this story go: we who are arranged, and the sun's blanket
fringed our own piece of exist, who talks like the trees are falling, and all day
goes like this, goes on like this."

The Shadow of the Object

I'm lying it was always already here
thickness of space can penetrate what touches things
water or light cut through walls
requiring time, my friends cut through reflection
vocal jump into the sea I'll apologize
the right name to chew on
music comes up to inhabit
you can have a sentence cordoning off the crowd
what nature can produce met everywhere
or anyway came back because I hit my head
in abject poverty do not crimp
obvious you are dead
I was able to whistle at both ends
levelled spit kept on happening
our fire would not come in the pool of darkness
the morning light resolves for a moment
constituting too much bad enough to do corners
the hot kids did something to us
tied with string some restaurant admitted free
falls down as simply as
mirrors beyond our control designate
seconds after lift-off
this table falling off a log
recycled in society is not a conscious energy
a final hope constructed meaning not knowing
the hills for the thousandth time really meant it
his hands just rounding things off
the probability of land
why do you have to ask me questions like that
a pain from a twenty year old knee injury
I'm a good president
it's still too dark if I set a gap
deliveries from other preventions a prodigal fear
formula attempts mistaken ways & means
an echo of a linked sunlight dead
exposed a folio of dried beams
meditations were taking me in a direction
you are a really good person

chewing and chomping where I would
the sense of song one destiny or fate will supplant
what may be material fact
there was something wrong in all this consciousness
the lilies of the field absentmindedly
to amuse and entertain
we wish to lull you to sleep
in the corner of your eye
with no more secrets you would come back
I would be your footprints
and you would have nothing to do
you would argue with what it's saying

bring this person
he went through these massive treatments
there's always this thing, remission
nonexistent — somewhere else
the subject and the object reconstellate
it's not absolute — what's the words to describe what can happen?
I have shrunk again
and often at dawn, having left it out all night, I bring it in
it matters little to what disjunction
the shining parts what is said

Let things come to rest upon a momentary presence of.
Or that you think things over, is "over" in them.
   Integrating fragments (oil pump)
          gap trust of hand.
      where the bulk of things find.

come toward test apron, excuse me, had prawn.
had a caramel camel.

the apples welcome guests you trust
the rough semblance
crowded that sugar bowl medium
for each gate pajamas shoulder repertoire
make habits reasoned
with loopholes
washcloth covering my sex
oh delta, foliate keystroke
other I thought my skin purple
subway history
everything is sweep porch sweet assemble
result of pen and thought happiness
when I melt that habit
whole ghosts of remote fool me
ought to swing my arms
more my whole body
point attention amory nor lie with action
and whole chain
(Add that to the list)
thins into melody the sound I polish
no basic task will disembody

Let things come to rest upon a momentary presence of me.
Or that you think things over, is "over" in them.
Integrating fragments (oil pump)
gap trust of hand.
where the bulk of things find.

come toward test apron, excuse me, had prawn.
had a caramel camel.
my concern.

I keep passing repetitively through these our pages.
Think your way out of that, its possibility
propels perhaps burns as an end, perhaps phenomenon
an outright lie. If a writing occurs, enacts its place
as a phenomenon in one's life, it holds/encompasses,
"slumbers at the edges of intention" (Steve Benson).

personality with all the pinpoint attention
of children's emotions is in your memory
you find it's kind of hard, neither truth nor lie
words occur crammed with action
the substance of life breaks up my whole chain

thick padding of your stuff that is free

It's more than just a window
different persons within this person
they're whole people, potential multiples

these weren't mythical images
image bent over street
unintelligible
that familiar order beyond their speech
forcing a gesture of help
parallels (not bad aspect)
anyone who's going down
incomplete action
"It's not displacement but relocation"
it becomes meaningless to other people

Looking in the mirror, when I tilt my head up or down,
I see someone I recognize to be my everyday self — his
reflection appears more-or-less constant, has constancy.
If I level my gaze, the person looking back at me is
another creature altogether, an absent alien from "my"
daily comings and goings. Eyes broader, complexion
brighter, features a purer composite of genders.

He withdraws from you or draws you into.

debris the next convention leaves flaws between. floats knees. propels
the palms brush by words as an end, an outright lie. its possibility
totems, yielding light in the read debris. ear letter that leaves by
words gone wild and still ship that line things. shape that in inside.
slow pastel side propels knees within that. pastel round thud heard
ringing. slaw that graphite lay. hip on side says hat. or if the ink
burst. knees streetlight. big sandbox gone wild — empirial curve in
the read road secure, red roving in. that slow ship inside that finish,
rises in that line compounding that one below.

the read ship that knees within that hip on sandbox. that slow ship
below one that roving in lays knees as an end. palms debris. ear totems
ringing shape that yield divide all space between that finish emphatic
think ears lathe. music of the sugarcoated. in these glaze leaded
shape below those that yielding lathe.

the intelligence be broken
and the heart laid bare

warmth of an intimate day thought between them. where the emotions scale
off and intercourse and sleep has a ripped ear. I walked in and found you
in bed. the lights flicker on and off in my mind. I can't remember what I
read. and so we agreed to place it outside us, an evening deferred, so
that it might not constantly interrupt us in the search for its meaning.

A book of deepening the beds

A book of the little beginnings of mischief

A book of the various movements
  passing through channels of various forms

A book of diverting from preventing

A book of the lowest level which can be
      found in the current of the surface

---

it was there for me, whether it was
intended or not
you had somehow made a conclusion about
that manifests — which doesn't mean
the same thing, how it manifests
I don't think it's out of thin air
a man or a woman, or the obscurities
benefit *kind of* comprehended,
holds them down to their place
you think because it's *your* sensitivity
could mean increase or decrease
to negotiate was too abstract
will not mind drowning the expense
the reader may well feel controlled
is not a biological need
a message and flow
      error I can't make out

Falling Away

falling elevator
outside elevator shaft exists
at different times
space is fluid
plus you should know
rectangularity
fantasy to have natural cause
not directly complex
genital reflection
the obvious
to put forth some effort
vulnerable
on the way into work
that interest radiates
pushed a bus aside
with my hands
these words are our woods
what we are lacking
can't remember
back where things were
moved through objects easily
a common criticalness
myself in pajamas with no pants
interlude on the subway
someone in the building
the burner in my mind

how that functions for you

that this future is here
you weed that hard contact
have possibility
in the fact of things
will change all that

Listening standing lengthening. Each new day's discrete sequence fundamental walked in a circle into this activity. An afterword cold bones something not righting that other manifest that keeps slippage takes from who would keep with a perspective that curves the subject you are in memory when you were opening inside eyes responsive public to locate notes where it looks like supplies continuing all them words gone home and set aside this movement doesn't surprise security the name you call, and with consent the polluted waters otherwise dry and I believe the truths and untruths performed for you the access warmth of our bodies and forming household implantations makes it easier and worse we walk there and square deals. I burn my fingers retrieving the bag of lemon zinger tea from the bottom of the cup. What a difference it is to sit here sadness relish the day measured accommodation because unpriced sound as it burns by lips hesitate my attention is a waste now it's ashen it's a white door we cannot see without coming back shadow overhead permanent reservation handloom turn around and face happy smiles and joy outside my discipline.

List	Listen	Listening
fund	fundam	fundament
bone	bones	bones som
take	takes	takes fro
you	you ar	you are i
to	to loc	to locate
gone	gone h	gone home
name	name y	name you
beli	believ	believe t
our	our bo	our bodie
wors	worse	worse we
bag	bag of	bag of le
it i	it is	it is to
unpr	unpric	unpriced
it's	it's a	it's ashe
over	overhe	overhead
smil	smiles	smiles an

Imagination and spirit passed away in the Form,
        to stitch yourself to it.

we will break the knees in the landscape
do we have to?
it radiates from its control the inconsequence
lists these things I don't know
It is mixed
because to struggle by
stroke after stroke
some unfriendly excess or imbecility
or is affected with egotism? or if he apologize?
or thinks of his dollar?

"None of this has to happen"

"you say that as if you've memorized it"

"everybody is to blame, but you"

———————————————◆———————————————

Like a ball of coloured wool the young tiger lies in the grass,
stretching his broad paws far out in front of him, and observing the
world with curious eyes

The hairs stand up impertinently on the little cranium

Again the little dromedary's soft lips rest on my hand

The Wise Spacemen

I wish we could share more readily
the geography through orbit
come to appreciate each other & know more about it

I have seen a lot of evidence
of destruction on earth
there are no dividing lines
there are no nations
except for selfishness and greed

if I should ever happen to die, got the midnight train
I wish I had lived a little longer
I'll read your other palm

I have set my heart on honesty, distrust my talents
these disorders that hesitate and fall

There's always more. Or it seems like there's always more there.
The distance to my fellow man is for me a very long one. An intricate
entrophy, the here end and now resting languidly, adds to the light
from eyes an extra light. Even if it was you at the beginning, seem
closer — an oscillation that insists on something.

the avenue my arms are held out toward

an identity maintained by style over there

Per Them Reconcilia

Mortal imagine what m the poi paralel
For ins blooms
but the escape are as man be prey up this of man
the spr in the mutabi course,
becaus who be tence
c late fo fond b
had no her w both o worth Keats them,.
You m as a Platon conseq or sac
and p I am n be so

———————————◆———————————

"How does this story go: we who are arranged, and the sun's blanket
fringed our own piece of exist, who talks like the trees are falling, and all day
goes like this, goes on like this."

Mown Stain Seed

                    ways of a number of them there
              the difference is spreading in giving
                    cast off what we want
              listening standing lengthening
        and that one from there liquidated my letters
              I was really interested in between
        other things seeing myself
                    a fraternity of patrilineal
              sending them away
                    some grammar blindfolded can I
        be normalized
                    the injustices
                    give up your ego
        each new day's discrete sequence fundamental
              grass phone seen as clogs, ending
        walked in a circle into
                          this activity
        I have found the answer words walled in
                    a long interval of carefulness
        no distinguishing signs   or sign of that
                    desertion between one window and another

Funny Appendix Verbal

the whole thing, the dark side of pop.
publicized styles and selves "between
our daily life & the great work"
dimly perceived push through curtains
to privacy "two or three dozen tombs."
an inflexible pace a path laid
straight over.
let them wallow of a thinking weight
greeting, kiss or handshake.
little singing thumb-knuckle.
another writer imagining you in his book about a writer, you,
writing about yourself as in another's book, inside of hers, that you, inside of
all that, have stolen ideas from yourself.
mistaking my middle finger beneath black bread
for clinging white butter.
the wash from that lit wick.

a line inside blackness and ringing, black and white, the white
pastel. the shape of the ear heard roving. the stillness seeps com-
pleting the chartreuse. the hands of the land and words begin to
give. the letter the silence rises in that line. the moisture of
a pair of eyes. read roving in round for red. thread read roving
thud. read slaw red thud slow over an open book. and pastel round
chartreuse, the colors use. graphite soul. the head the people leaves.
and within that finish the shape of the ear red thud. read silence.
chartreuse roving within that line. the letter s of shadow or b.
draw a line inside the shape of. the shape of the ear heard ringing
in the head. that ship slipped into shape. and within that finish.
and within that line things. and in that that leaves.

puddles, and glue, in hesitation.
the "effect" of, or distance to.
or nature and language
render the concrete.
the cocker spaniel umber spoon burnt.
"togetherness"
the promise of distance taken.
an ancient legend, "god knows where we're headed"
sponged on the horizon.
cellophane specks of rust threads.
pencils & the sharpened dust.
the goddamn distance. the economics
of imagination. translation of dispersed
grassy clumps on loamy black slopes.
echolalia upon the support of the page.
a paranoia of
unfortunates.

Theft of Services

They can barely stand by themselves
people who told me I could move on
everything I see isn't that clicked-in
the results still mushroom
willing to move planet wide open
forget carbon dioxide
everything old western newspaper shivering
suggestion in your pocket gimmick
the intimate in a kind of fixed intelligence
disasters in a frayed suit
reparation, identities as articles you understand?
cutting off this curious emotion
its silent peripheries regimen
can procure them for you
let me nurse my baby first
these were still "vegetarian" times
rejoice in this tiny canker
we can always find time to die
not necessity a poet of renunciation?
a private person
whose work could be either accepted
or rejected
chatting and joking antedate these drugs
this is just what I enjoy

Self Trees Feet Dream

a message and flow
error I can't make out after the step
figuring pleasure who believed that good
separate as chaotic given sense of
into the thought speech and perfect phrase
song texture won't give
corner drawn across it country power career
running dreams irreversible balance
disperses would want to live
sheltered like this
semblance flattened against
doesn't get its chance
refuses without relation that of attitudes
but it was also permitted toward the artist
even monsters like music
cows looking in point of view he was smiling
the claw whom I love angular and square
satan takes a holiday
one another reverse that without change

always some yourself reading "satan has
so much more a grip on the people"
our great hope is particular entities
"I had an acquaintance who watched her husband
choke to death at dinner, not knowing
what to do. Now here's a worse tragedy..."
all the "animals in the street"
one-way ticket accepting all comers
there is another example of futility
the city the mind never fixed?
sense of song clear of cars had to take notice
don't look so well or sound
almost no skill involved haunts all people

Black Plateau

for Jackson Mac Low & Anne Tardos

Miserable John of shadow sensuality
Whose vacant locks at a convent
Wall turning my hand to it taking
The infidel childhood completed
Erudite esquires podium filch effect
Dough lack knowledge neck knelt
Dry tender button this debacle knob
Awful sunk weeks difficult foster
Leg by thick hinge poinsetta ahoy
Ratified jab you feral ruffians
Eye pads curb or fade deep psalter
Ash sifted quick opera zeppelin arts
Faithfully fall off of fiduciary
Duffle toad piddle bent budget retread
Bronze volume burnt box vaccinated
Kept hecklers walk doubt ate
Inchoate incoherence like cousins
Chip deaf glands aid johns erupt flan
Rear oil ruminary ergo quietude rut
Tiptoe over cyprus pry zinc voice
Decible matza cab-n-belly-up deafen
Trek toward skin cagey ewe cabinet
Shasta wafers fizzy salt teapot
Page slop judgement wasn't germane
Swerves through perpendicular sweet
Yellow figs sad sigh foul thieves
Stalker isn't liked wields urgent
Murmur aid pepper pouch yolk
Cigar death food birth face
Harnesses hard tequila sustenance
Forlorn beelzebub druid soap laden
Brew of thought can press sap from
Tofu stopped tweezers broomful
Military hegemony "Chief of men"
They choose to call my head
A cancellation, home as an asset
The devils in evening dress piety
Systems cold unification pools
Blunt of illogical composure echo
Big-headed juice joy behaviour
Locking horns intimately indirect
That is good that is gone
Pulsing dark adoration indissoluble
Unknown knots of "intentionalism"
Noiseless purchase measures inter
The individual the World
Unmarked observation driven through
Slams blurs semblances paroled
The strongest, the outer suburb
This volition is the one

and then another nothingness not standing up from
to think of lines
what happens on my own turf as it rests
still wet know this much stamina
a headache because you're to type
all this shards of assembled
bled in a shallow below
its root
residence
opposite reason
or truth country
speaking to whom god bless
those problems
a black absence of measure
ricers
of a semicontinuous mush
notin or a complete
sense
which shows
surreal — people are so weird
into the arena w/out
knowin

The American Sublime

I kept my hair longer for that job
than for that one. has come closer.
make them coexist together
without difficulty? getting supplies to people.
our living standard including foresight and judgment
gets into the atmosphere. no solid unbroken thought
ink to make. couldn't get around religion.
the past is really something.
there are a couple of white clouds
chemical like rocks and trees to make
read someplace men the web of spontaneity.
armies supportive and all
I suppose despair enough of the rest.
supplies continuing all them words
I take with me ears absorption in it.
a fairly straight mouth full of vowels
couldn't see enough, communicate, to most
of them there. seashore.
a big deal for yourself any-way integration
purposive in your thinking
will assist and encircle as dew.
long affinity within finite margins
the space they measure held in
layers of no more words casting long shadows
of a single sense. my body
lifting residue from the floor
in my hands. turning my head around
Euripedes gesturing. searching
in the rows full of misfit rabble.
they had read some books
so they felt that they were
new to him, unreal father at odds.
he thought he was the driver of a feeling
of home. the mother and father are shown
he was the driver of a feeling
in the house. the children sleep
stunned by the constant chat.
everyone drinks and smiles at everyone.
and the seasons were senseless.
and good fortune was contained.
though our attention and our lucidity
puts us in a class of our own
what if I did look up your trunks
and see it. the cocktail warms
his courageous mirror
to defense or aggression combatting
the void of imperfect statement.

I might be fooling you, pulling your leg, but
when I'm writing I'm sincere even when manipulative.
Even when I'm most personal in the right way.
But I don't know where this is leading. Maybe
it doesn't need to lead anywhere. I'm sorry
you're away and I miss you very much.

I have to be very careful now because I've
run out of correction tape. If I made a mistake
it stays. I wish you'd stayed but you couldn't.
I think I understand why, then know I don't after
it's explained. In the explaining everything takes
on a different color, I begin to see things between
us others never saw. They can't see now. I wanted
to pull everything up and take off. How it all
didn't matter didn't make sense anymore. I wanted
letters to say more, to explain things. Put
point by point those things were never said,
seemed to fall away before my pen. I was bitten
with forgetfulness. I tore up all our pictures.
I see now what a mistake it was — how I couldn't
get away from things that easily. How the secret
meaning of wishing each other's death came to
make more and more sense, and saddened by it.
Wondering how many times we've appeared in this
universe — would we find each other again. That
kind of insanity and unable to express one iota
of it. Becoming so clear it exploded
behind my eyes — it wrote words on paper I
can't understand. Exploded in my gut.

―――――――――――――――◆―――――――――――――――

paddled rooms
      customer's restraint   after midnight 12/10
        exhausting   till 1 a.m.
     deliberation of
   it doesn't matter to me
shadows within each groove of the brush
      something weird just happened
   patterned design of the bedsheet
      palm of my hand cut by the
          broken handle its stub
          of a cup
    parenthetical molding
      where's this shit come from?
      I don't understand
   one more little tiny bit coming out
the "v" shapes, the square "o's"
          equals signs
     flowers that remind me of bananas
          their ridges & black ends
   not a band saw but a rotary saw
          pyramids at all angles
    lifting the chin to the left with my left hand
      crack of vertebrae
   delicately moving books in and out
          on their shelves
    placing attention
          round mounds of shadowed
knuckles broken by the pens bell
      the garbage somebody will throw away
   you pollinate grass on
      the wall
    cluster hurry unclear to say no
  what it's wired to say loudly
   no that's worth it
    give it just a moment
  you've been saying this for years

Psychic Income

for D.R. Miller & Dave Barrett

Steak their tincture scarred suds
Quaff malt jersey shod cue off jelloed
Syllable debit plead fingers woo self
Cow town effort dill milk kong doodles
Ruckus her caesar additive shelter shat
Fall walks ellipsis montezuma guru
Pure jam diode ink da king bee arcane
Ink knelt bean dip dealt arts link ids
Dough enough angels fly high to lie
From warship lieu of shore babble I die
Civic bible police feud feds a few sap
Burn feak felt factile list locked all
Favor qua knicker snicker paid plenty plow
Choice buffalo refreshments orgasm seminar
Flabby plucked teeter first fancy oil
Off addled generator steak fudge plus
Dinero shovel shy a sloth beer sauce
Mod pen days jot old poe joy changeover
Angular shepard table beard butt bald bust
I can't let him eat them smelly fart
Flasks nothing snuff to pluck stirrup
Tao permit sold sands with potato salad
Ghastlike let diminutions asp pass advance
Inserting the promise of shapes dewey
Alcove soup alert kit lute kindle
Blame elision of the hunter's moist brocade
Mercury lid kill sour cobalt knuckle
Burly god survival skewed second plea
Knob in the mouth covered with dreams
"shoe" it from another linguistic angle
Self shambles its shares red skeleton
Clubs lower links necessity breaks
Two blocks worth of Wrigley Field
Varietal identity I can't remember them
Furtive peer napkin berth dour blink
Firewood asks me, "Not knowing what
You expect, made still dirtier waving
Q-tips makes me think for the corn
Spontaneous terraces begin to groan
Responsibilities you neglect peers
Avoid dingy alfalfa reunion weld duct
Pod folded peas turnstile smothering neck
Muscle dopey elbow daily whole hog plasma
Spot aerodynamic roof life telluride
Shelter riding cuffs wholesome colossus
Ghost lathe late be dial mode goddamn
Idaho dais putts sardinian velvet spuds
Mustard riddled fad aloe gallow spackle
Shoveling chairs poke walk da fake done
Shellfish a chunk from your cheek."

---◆---

To do what a person said he would do or had done a canopy I descend present ourselves to each other, weigh for them when canonized always that distance between stick my hand into the sea I said narrative that's the whole process cross the ocean landscape scroll a de-funct agency doctors and nurses the whole long terrible continuance changing color with the sun weren't home that evening that listening their adornments to sleep base of your brain salvage you'd stopped to think geography of colonized song stuck to the palate intellects discipline about the accuracy of their exports came so far to germinate. Even in the daytime blue high above who is only stoical thrust of beautiful my own loneliness difficult plastic seal into beads the rude at their jobs assumed not to be at ease in shelter scribble come back, stood in the place one with one in that word it is beneath that end turns an apartment the turbulent freedom sophisticated share in line. Mutual, but offer this forming limbs in motion talk about "the body" else perversion drink electric age in your heart trusting it seems silly a speck of sauce the whole poem doesn't burn as much as you should? Not one in this country is the resting? Out the window opening up the door the sunlight selves folded backing off values inhabits, finds it, doesn't care could ever hope for.

My mother's praise & my sweet little symbol

listening brain and mixed song

your heart sauce upon trusting

"I have no money because of the Lord."

You pressed the "reality button"
the fragility of falling in the reality of distance to the other

---

To keep these words in mind
                    and use them as a beginning.
                in the natural course
                        rhythms it hasn't yet sunk
                The narrator's lead us, heart in mouth
                        the rest disappears
                Almost makes me think their speech
                    is inflicted as a table of contents
                Playgrounds on breasts
                the pleasure of moving multiplication
                    Get your head out of the page
                that softness of the five o'clock sun

                The world kept coming
                        enticing the present sentence
                            splitting it
                    to quiet all the static sounds
                                around us.

embryo, what can I do before several people to be a house "peacefulness." as mine, shelf near the table cereal box filled my memory of easily, a daydream I had meeting, abstracted it was headless, the torso and limbs floating in space my mind. a kind of blown-up bag, organless inside, and my attention as "teats," of the body

The little creatures that have no words. If you just describe
what you see, you'll be sure to get there, you'll arrive in
the sphere of the things under the skin of your hands. My lips
freshly squeezed free from explanation. Highwire made to be
that children clutch up around burdenless beneath feet, two
parts of joy that one. Not altogether examining them before I
dismiss the flawless, regular very white line of perpetuity
to help possess, modify what relationship circles — the body
inter perpetuity to help process, modify in some way what the
poems inhale, make probable touching lips my face can't eat.

Full of Another Blue Hand Writing

Someone who would take care of that part of things. Like crests, crests
of air by sinking buoys the doors yesterday and tomorrow fact to the
ground said the trees pass through the hand for my heart. Don't invest
in the first person the time the space "I just wanted to kill everybody
I was working with." Now get up and drive a soft landing. Happiness and
blessing, lost gourds and spent soils cells of the clock coronary
complications a magazine falling one by one sets his pack to the other
voices I would listen to. If I can keep that from their municipal trust
as bare as his own future beautiful scattered life's like tht all
round — things follow, I also remember you, an aristocracy *roots* the
semi-fascist population on the frozen filed automatic rifle I don't
know if there is anything lacking. Water-level traces be such a damn
nuisance, the displacement like that, nightmare demonstration on
Washington rust unbearable arrangement the recession not mended weighed
in addressed as inside it history of the moon delectation the reader
ran away with ability striking an ethic context of being alone or of
dismantling yourself sweet day competence is lost like that. A soft
landing, happiness and blessing is not changed and here lovely
afternoons, or other "permissions" has that instinct sticks to the eye
every light at any point verse-line silences, sweaters hugging, end of
the cave ovation before it comes to tell of. The departing soldier
counts by one the door not hurt teach you a lesson summer and fall a
bomb which tears the heart out. I respect their silences. The precision
of your sentences composes a colony of black spots.

drive a soft landing through the hand for my heart doesn't
invest in the first.

Flying over the delta in the translucence of their

sentence playing hangman be good
unfastened screen
sunning to a word is signal or someone
lies between (from) bend out
the other end falling further
light the finality of that
not ahead of not standing
each sentence
its felt window
intercedes a spray across the inside
assistance after
how the things seen
came to be together
living together had assembled
or had been assembled there
or had developed *there*

Your Calendar of Sentiments

for Dan Davidson

hostile to the umpire
the printers ink
swimming in the pool

writing around your labor

the turns, stops, & lingering
shoulder the presence of

to build up. to listen. to listen in me.
the corner of this room blesses this
one cloud-creaking-sound.
dark green always h.
whatever was is
crumpled so very over under the sea.
an opening which
manipulates variables of.
successive generations
monitoring this word
an external intravenous chocolate
its conical cap
the death of something
caught with a pen.
consciousness is butter
of antinomy.
exceptionally smooth
I know they had gone
the sublime
skims the real memorial.
prey upon one another
only if it masks sense.
unconcealed overcome
fallible denial of all
that men call leisure.
'the ardor of your brain'
spectrum
the untouched page
erritory of chance
growing beside
eyes leveled here.
hostile to the umpire
the printers ink
swimming in the pool

writing around your labor

And Their Space Be Gone

surf ace eat urican sacut of atath
his om unity hecoash asiven
hings wean do kino come hesion
yocut fir cost albelt ollow
eat cites ensevege ration wat
reyur lectoff icial sigasown ancer
herg bicidfomemo ryllide eep yoof heseets
mens a shitone lees awee harp gene coutfi
are axed bod our o wizen aim or heshdow falarger
todom innate dot o ether tore emerse ilbecom ingfull
I can say cueoff at omrenensi
eat surge aceeture thin wean
them host comoon kin flow the reads

figurations. take me with you when you start.
our daily doubt. vestiges strew
pull us down to loneliness. does not do.
disturbance charms my incantations, elegance
afternoon upon the keyboard, a melody to
shield with wounds. the trouble all over America,
escape from. cannot digest it.
violent shore speaks softly the long unfeelingness.
delivers couldn't care less. crumbs of whimsy
implement and act. the disclosure resembles
integration of the past without place. unkempt
total affluence of a young man. an allegorical
lawn floods one another's separation; words
reaching without requisition
the dust of their feet. the angle
extinguishing their arena. reason
applauded out of heaven. how sensible
that form remains in place without lips.
the pen can indite passage from the world.
without counseling the letters
squeeze them all together. interpret the verse
an excellent ladder. door and wall
altogether speech. the waves I see on that shore
pinned all together cannot help you in.
sets you off.
with money you make a nice young living.
take care of itself.
leave the house dry in the mouth.
I wish I wasn't so dead
I'd tear you limb from limb.
that a clear line appear.
that I be allowed that much space.
between an elite that interprets
what I understand to belong to me.

word that produces all images.
these hundred comprehensions walked softly.
"moved" by how, where. aim shadows
immersed in nonsense surge of whose ascension to
the massive enough world hurled down.
answer salvaging leftover community of known and
unknown mutability people cut off smaller
ride of your house. I saw you saw
enough word till anger load in divide
cut down candour. gut of teeth or
fête erasures. fare reprehensible few
curving up into living a relaxed body your own size
named for you. great cities a great distance.
protection where no one protects.
pity's a cheat. coming around the shift
you can't be where you are
and there's too much big pro-detection.
heads swear yes (or) kingdom come
your will thin won. defenseless fated
does property mean fat lingual
I has labored for vermin, bent back
conformity to a social pen?
cryptic outfit bowel of the earth
issuing magic oracle threshold
smothered with one's democratic leisure.
words taste good here. unpigmented, gel.
a field full of folk thinned.
its alterity place I put down words
hookers green. eager to dominate
your passionate but impartial love.
the cup or the dish in my shadow fought when it met
whose line? I'll have to wear this armor.
harbor deeper than any intellectual
I love you and you love me. who has killed more women,
children, and men. more choice in
everything. circumstance and a sweetness
a wide place stronger a serenity
for any silent resemblance, not more care.

lean dream reads less hostile typed.
cycles off at receipt. bubbling of the green.
each bill defers.
many people and Things they open.
many cities wait until they return. difficult
how it happens getting that out
forge it natural. taste of it
in their mouths.

the stagehand who made one appearance
during the scene not between them
dimming of lights, the actual light
a streetlamp shadowed against a wall
can't think of how to put it
the prop removed, and that seems strange
you could say this is the replay
a performance of a similar
perhaps shared confusion standing
gesturing with beer bottles in both hands,
I don't know what to make of
my appearance at that precise moment
signals, how words begin to to give
it's convoluted and personal
believing somehow that any of it, meanings,
I can't say aren't deliberate
something's winning someone's attention
or affection attentive to these things
how they affect,
doubts and confidences spill out,
recover with humour
the whole show deliberated
staged so that the flaws don't show
reading "more in my brain"
attempts to acknowledge them
I'm having difficulty?
adjust onrush of words I ply
he says he knows,
but the whole thing what he's doing
knowing — deliberately to reach
psychologically off what reasonable person
has seemed inexpressable

tap in to let go.
to learn to ease withdraw from something
than personal. words fallen below the blue line.
I was just somebody else, some stranger, and my
whole life was a haunted life, the life of a ghost.
it's because they could be the reverse of you
venture into the regions their confused version
once they are outside of it but everywhere extended
and had nothing to do with sounds. also slow
they aren't afraid or altered consciousness
down, become a child again you want to cry.
running, repulsing, okay after a group of little girls.
refuse promises of the absolute between me
and the rest of the world.

meager grass. rest. water soft as air.
waves in a pond after a pebble. nothing called language
can go this far. this is ours.
great wood. doors usefulness. criterion
song over the land.
an imagination? choose self?
recognize your theft? you periods and commas
learn how. blood braided then undone
open our eyes. children won't stop talking.
holds their tongues. I'll remember your walk
welcoming benefit of beautiful things.
a vast tobacco field and last cigarette.
that they went away that way
but never sacked easily nested in their own
slanted homes. planting commendation,
making allegory from a continent whole as pardon.
an american panic — suntanned, orangery,
pensive, fallow, intense, can take any paradise
within. "the house is empty... but for myself,
imperfectly perceived." penetrations
toward intricate delight, what cells protect
and disallow, terrifying
emerge in boats to these openings.
"now that we've got love"
glued together. sinking feet into an elegance
an afternoon descending in that attitude
you had written, which reverses.
shoe-shine parlor in father's clothing shop.
entertainers, sellers right in its middle.
I believe my rabbi, dentist and telephone.
Time Magazine. manner of. music of.
real and unreal house launches into rotation
a seasonal illness term of utility
purely automatic (or, if you prefer *do* intervene).
then sound, not the object. an artificial
echoed same world hibernation shutting
the constants of mystery I am held by the story
of my own body. the interior sleepless
in his hand, no entrance or exit.

It's what you might imagine a dead man would feel if he could tell
you what death is. Explain how he ended up there and tell the
beginning of his story. How things have changed and what's important
to him now. If he could provide any ideas as to why men throughout
history continually dwell in it. Justify its significance, its
changes with the experience. Does death signify anything to the dead.
That is, it's not so much death I want you to tell about, as it is
the experience of moving from one life to another. The snow in
perspective under the stars. The speakable geography of anxiety
describe. The world that is to please the world.

puddles, and glue, in hesitation.
the "effect" of, or distance to.
or nature and language
render the concrete.
the cocker spaniel umber spoon burnt.
"togetherness"
the promise of distance taken.
an ancient legend, "god knows where we're headed"
sponged on the horizon.
cellophane specks of rust threads.
pencils & the sharpened dust.

myth of the not her blood

"inside the between that is turning"
— *Gertrude Stein*

through your tending themselves
the mirrored anxieties a town a room
clamor for so much heat
foreground to be fed with new nights
dismantles our patience
dream yourselves sisters I've no earth
arranged so that pain pulls in
upon these difficulties and offer my appeal
enlightenment accuracy
no generalized effectively regime
social other centers essay
reproduce everyone objects blows
it's good inside your mouth
your vain lateral borders
no distinction of sex
love's power your questions
the unseparated limbs of intuition soft flex
paper think against the fat
real idiots rolling on the edge

your transparent sponge brain
fabulous discipline, the endless drillings
language stuck to the palate
of houses explains and accompanies a car
a young girl lies stretched out
nobody asks for our participation
I'm a fool
to move before you
I must tilt upon the pressure
a pencil execute and adjust
subterranean mesh of their touch
immediate speech
going to bed, making love
tossing loneliness of many nights
still green & fresh
turn and look at what you see
photochemical dispatch
moral mutation
of digression not swing
that total location of the self
is not dead in me
your body will haunt mine
dance of your nipples in my mouth

in the evening a smile
I'll remember your walk
will not say her name
and you periods and commas
tell me what time is
this harvest on your skin
music too slow
Wednesday I am still waiting
nothing comes
the cool conditioned air
was in the rhythm of thought
soft, soft flush
is the only one he ever talks to
even as they fill the air
it moves up and down
seems dark and smoky
lamp dimmed
all the vows of love once promised
but faintly shows
they love you
they love you is distinct

this is all about what atonement
I am learning to feel
the words have changed, held back
you will say they saw themselves
the paragraph inside me
and the other planets
which mattered very much
(and which you feared would disappear)
they learn
"I want to go from here with you"

my heart is breaking
ellipsis padlocks slake off
falls walk aggravates shelter
loosely wrought manifestos
I stay here in the woven light
my life in that text
all the names of my absent friends
an assembling of signs
the smug guns, trained on
the whites of their eyes
and the scent of pine needles
in our hemisphere
I'd like to meet a good friend
to come along and talk
the sweet body rubbed
getting larger and more excited
I'm talking too much
my heart is not here

dreams full of mothers and fathers
lines functioning
cast into what you meant
read magazines
the chaotic rank and still position
emptier than ever
"but I was always away..."
cease to administer
binding referendums, bankruptcy intent
the sad splendour and play
beautiful belly path for dinner
the space between us
this island of Manhattan
sunning the insides of
its clues
sliding down the milky way
a nothingness, but darker weight
hard and soft at once

people still think with the history
which has already past

in a rain tent
kind of a meat umbrella

"the imperfect is our paradise"
end of the Alphabet washed clean

"dark here in the driftings"
the distance at which we hold one another
translate the lines
little red sausage person
white wine and peppercorn stubs for arms
eyes interfering with vision, broken pump
& attention to what people do
flexures, hepatic, splenic, sigmoid
free from four defects
layers of matte gelatin
experimental stations
the fastened world written in
a hopeless time
rain-filled tree holes
our strung intentions of stone forts
literatures brought together
together are pure invention
I am always astonished in your presence
this whole surface of daylight
my retreat

my self come to get me
their mirrored faces locked
its pipes benediction

a sort of permanent transparency
fascinated me because I could see myself as the tune

manuscript pages covered with
"question this page"

and my room fossilizes
descendant of continuance

the final adjustments
raised up out of his grave

the night's constellations
the body of the small point

the always unequated remnant
pushing shopcart for bottles & cans

we will visit the sun
of that sentence in my hand

the varicolored joy of our eyes
the sandy witness of your bed
the results of its division
hands full of smooth flesh
so there you are
who held no property
and stretching & yawning
through this industrial wasteland
calm in the circles
perhaps nearly dead
the soft spot
where the silence is
where the simple lights grow
if I move down above
her legs against mine
what solitude I've finally inherited
dark adoration
the place my tongue has found there
in soluable unknown knots of
made new
runs on in my head

moving into the 90's
I thought there was something to their word
I thought I was trying
my vision keeps referring to
your conversation
in forgotten or misplaced rooms
in the sweet darkness
the heavens ceaselessly scan
this is a song in someone's public
emotionality
the beautiful belly
the alternative in the outer shell
the pen dent on thighs composed
a few months obliterate
maybe no luck for a long time
in all the nerves clarify
the kind of light I have in my head
only care for grass or sea
or peace

lying on my back on the white dust
visualizing it in your mind
a propriety of attention
a night covered with jewels
on the sleeper's head
mineralized in the moonlight
unemployed persons
one of your stray thoughts
about to grasp the knob someone
has just handed you
the present thing all sexual display
the language between
and the things it names
mental face containing market research
unable to receive love
another project for the heart
the world's waste of light

Who kisses the theme away from this farm, prefigurations shoved over
emplacement? I need to. The heroine of my vision unleashing no surprise
to the leasing of our program. The exhibition of similar evenings
bringing profit to the crowd. You slip around about that, but something
must be proclaimed. Perceiving that the instrument was not singing
alone, you counter-balance. The other children play in a smell of their
own. Getting rid of reality experiments, you project if I'm willing to
give it up. Don't understand a word of it. The day lengthened by
artificial light. In that space independent of influence from the rest
of the planet, surface textures continue to ape and fold. Each pair
coming from opposite sides of the stem.

placing attention
round mounds of shadowed
knuckles broken by the pens bell
the garbage somebody will throw away
you pollinate grass on
cluster hurry unclear to say no
what it's wired to say loudly
no that's worth it
give it just a moment
you've been saying this for years

creak of pulleys hauling cement
from the street below
— Giancarlo!
the beautiful shape upon
which one might lounge
rock of alley's awning
meant rumour
treats hello joined angular
happenstance pummel
watches onerous weight
languor
cure of ways warning
others murder ants
hell allows angels to eat
melancholy standards
ensue ape
eight raspberry cheese
hatches liquor
warm urinal

things that don't matter to me
don't matter to me
I'm forced to tell you
breathing and sentient, open-eyed
the perfect self identity
the poles of pure life move on
"no one, has loved the west I came into"
the sense comes over me
the cents, simple pun bullet in her brow
the blanket of the phallus
the carnival they rent off
an unvisited garden of childish geography
melons at the well
you want to be the master
not of verses, but of the light
of what you say and do
to walk the perfect lawn
carry beauties in your heart
till the day you die
I said narrative
the whole long terrible sun

the credits on the television
so many constellations held out
take precedence
men are fools to invest
beneath the singular
it's what happens
you can see it in our eyes
in a room listening to this shape
semblance stands back up
clothes hold still in holes
the word of stuff a dirt
pressure through optic throat
things won't rest

dark or just enough light
made palpable, swallow that

the brain can't run out
for adoration

when you love someone
speak from there

when you have written
let it all sit

anything more to see
doesn't keep

slip in through my ear
and there we'll shelter take

rub your pus-sy
against my e-rec-tion

kick gently
when the rain beats down

drop raw my banana meat
deep in your locks of scent

your june is over & all your
beauties asleep

a body to be caressed
no word can expose

the poet uses poetry
we no longer know where

tangerine terminator
my will is simple

I am one of the citizens
very few people are free

what is constantly on the move
smear of sky on a hunk of earth

short steps from the shore
the way everyone goes away

lights flash off in the distance
in the swell of a deep sea

into the trees of the future
alchemical mind's heady brew

this makes me wonder
where the country is

the story about life and death
the black things the lines

an unleveling of thought
comes from the open places

put things together
between thoughts

a signification
outside it, being part of a system
fixed only by the concurrence
that stands in opposition to it
each of us goes out in a morning
that's behind an ending
I'm more interested in verbs
our shed chamber
I don't know how to end
the whole society would lose
their wheel and rotate
in the chaotic ocean

Rice soul will come see
not seeing but just seeing

we are glad you could come
it's impossible not to

leave no footprint on the rock
the city breaks in

I lived it until this day I do
we dance on hills above the wind

when a juicy baby comes around
it pushes your buttons

Now, this is your beer
Which way did you come?

and let him die by inches
visit a fine passage where the action is

put a word in front of another
which version you were going to see

like the rising and falling of
no more work remains

his ears their ears become familiar with fables
that he may fill it of himself

reason and intellect have departed in madness
to an end all the secrets of speech

silence is the sign of death
you are fleeing from the silent one

between the dead and the living
what the other imagines each means
seeing and feeling and self
it's speech at the interface of
focusses most of what we know
that each being is at each moment
its own specific end
"sit still and write your thesis"
a haze echoes of "common sense"
parallel purpose
a "kinder, gentler nation"
a perfectly closed labial fumbled
this is the only way it seems
like something implicit
listening brain and mixed song

what we take from it
keep cutting across
this half-world, my body
both light and heavy with you
the only lasting part
your heart sauce upon trusting

the physical conditions of life
for principles
birds had dropped or had nested
may be your emblem
but to be a hotel keeper
if all the others had not died
who can sit and write as if nobody says
move in it a city hall that we try to break
these poems will not be revised
or didn't think
the heart's motion without sound
I was also in those I send
I feel close to you at that party
a certain quiet made us die
I'll let you know
these are all really the effects of dis-
course they come *after*, in the solitude
of a circle or a straight line
can't see inside
to see what one sees
the one's loved trying to make the room whole
they pretend to be detached
I run through the water, show off
shadow unloyalty

the book not seen
what will you do with the one you love

take this shadow produced
by my present activity
"I don't know who I am"
"the circling air"
"the meaning of change"
have only themselves as grounds
it ought to be enough
the whole scene is empty
but somehow I was left
decorating my hair, worrying
its shape into the trees

the replication of care

for Hannah Weiner, Steve Benson, Abigail Child

The Replication of Care

"We leave with those leaving arrive with those arriving
leave with those arriving arrive when the others leave"
—*Tristan Tzara*

memory flies out the window
that's the first thing to remember
the old gentleman chasing after someone
hands merge
burn on the page from a matchstick
illimitable
spongy smack of radials

Give me some pleasures of
the outside
that it changes deaf to
in the rain-slicked
dim lamp blue noontime
a horn blows
morning and evening people

Trust am I to eyeing myself
be attractive flooding the room into a revolution
the philosophy pollen to filter
tilt over repeated mistakes
don't want to let go, & that *poem?*
Let the advent sum now 3 days on the
page heat like summer's sultry sun lies

There was a lot of space between
these thoughts when *I*
experienced them
motorcycle *burning* rubber
That gate closed tight
Hubcap, closed door, laughter
get moving

To balance words
do verticality shown
it actually *is* a *cappuccino*
What would happen to want to follow
concrete of this page
To slip out stands on with the previous
sounds I must understand below

hear in this frail
invention I won't wrestling make me
actual light
can't adequately express
water touching
evaporated all
push around attendants

Imaginary kingdom
spontaneous slow-measured purchase
Noiselessly entered
Mouth slightly bent round
the earth
Corners none of their business
the public...

tell people much more than their minds
After his second voyage, it was Isabella of
Castille who gave him the money
it was built by Hannibal in 200 B.C.
The public detection of your decay,
the other fellow
(un)clothed with the other

Conditions adapted to individual existence
on the side of the page
The impartiality lets hard sell aid
This propaganda
the deliquescence of instruction
The revolutionary synonym societal efficiency
content on a Third Reich

By its side he found out
life scarcely together came
Took trouble with words
inner harbour to be looked out of
That was what I wanted to tell you
the passionate
just resemblance make known

do not turn against one another
Men's voices holding-down
the neighborhood
do not turn against one another
one's moving
Helicopter flying overhead
"Goddamn (something) right
in the... heh, heh, heh"

"...the rules for the replication of pattern
guide their dreams
safely into our dreams"
Lakes of oil
waiting for spring
He would soon be asleep
in the fall

"The United States can do that with The Word."
                    television commerce
                          Angels
                                singing through my bedside
                    "You consume your happiness?"
          the idea is keeping people further away
                          away from

Everyone makes one another a target
                    he knows
                    I am watching tv
                    the trailing arc
          entrained over the surface of the ice
                    It is a perfect present,
                          A love through glass

          It pays to be big on milk
                    administrative competence?
          The "confusing mosaic" of the middle east
                    U.S. content 72%
                          Merely the literal translation

                    "Set Yourself Free"

We are entering the 21st Century
                    concerned about your neighbors?
          You wrote about
                          people & their language
          and believed it was with them
                    a Writer begins
          her particular novel phrase

"Let me go home with these
                civilized people"
Feel wonderful and successful
                in your own body!
            Spectacular Soft Flex
                that's what motivated me
        Some of that thumb-sucking therapy

            A big skinny thing
            it's really spooky, it's got
                    "Paradise" in the title
        A guy was hanging on a pole
                and bouncing from threads
                Another white suit story?
        they forswore him in the future

            In Park Slope — casual corner
            A log on the fire in Pleasantville
        "why should I be alone"
                impossible to not be completed
    "Who the hell is this?"
            "I gotta do what I gotta"
            "That is my mission"

Swerve on the censure spoken
            shelf raided of fat donut custom
        Reception pooped on the rent
            sizeable rupture not idle play
                the insurance we were on
                Tenure lotto prize
        the warring lines of letters

The ether poured at command
                    and pretend to swallow
          Limit at a loss
                    Politics of value
          It really does
          look like a man walking down a hill
          You have

                    a man walking down a hill
          There is a low drywall of competence
                    for staying on the frame
                              by consent
          The frost is the recession
          All that need & desire
                    Because you (and I) do not divide

          Your smiling purity
     speak on the banks of Lethe
               implant the graft
               that he shall never know
               And the music of that place
          without leaving a trace
               Arguing for something I don't

     In the middle weaken
          won't run be afraid of
          accustomed to
     A tent shape perceived upon the paper
                    on which he writes
               impossible to not be corrupted
               Field fall foul

the "common path"
or "experience" ("for the few")
            the level of your diction
half way into each other
                        phonemes of the requisite
self-contained knowledge — "our own measure"
                        "waits for the price to fall"

            Undressing
'this soft book comes into my mouth'
            consigned ancient respectability
I look for something & the engine is adding up:
            "You will get an award from me
                        of discomfort;
            or replica of it."

            shadows tip over shifting ground
We look at the process
            and at the same time
listen to readers glad to hear you
            answering questions and asking them
The beginning and end of each way
            the necessary operations

are destined to have a large future
            He sees light comes out of water
    "It doesn't seem
                        to me to need anything
                                    absent"
            it has no care for your presence

About the Book

My mind belongs in the expression
my thoughts world. I could write that
another way...

Now think they said. This is
the first room to talk on the level.
        Like I've parked
a dominant status eyeing an emotion
lost to consciousness
in the bathroom of tradition. Everything
in its name.

How did things smoke the wild ones
advertisements articulated in?

I am in a wander. Earnest reader
writing is a *wilderment*.

To follow the path of continent social revelation slightly levitate different places, not fictional as that nothingness we follow is of no importance. *Self shambles its shares,* voices dwell on lips become recognizable turning my limbs in manufacture and ideas of taught to lie still. To "find" my thought and its expression became abstract property — alternate composition trusted doubts about any method capable of wounding reading strategies and contexts of expropriation detailed between different raised edges — I, you, he, or something else — understands don't even think permanency when it is this [the rhythm of what came before, after]. An opportunity no longer to make stingy granting them names, something other than a name.

relaxation to keep awake
a first call muffled in
how I adjust when it isn't
solace though desireable
mistaking reaction for a just
response — think to taper it off,
time and space existing in
perceptions of senses felt
in their contacts to
a world believed to be real
        caught in prolificacy
(to send signs forward — to tend

Is the knowledge which you have of yourself a direct
perception of yourself by yourself, or do you get it from
something else?

It reminds me of something I'm in.

A sort of wobbling transparency so that we can converse
with some appreciation of each other's position.
we do really need to know what we want.   tongues slipping
we entertain ourselves with wonderful forms, a strenuous
exercise in sensitivity and tenderness.   Aerial.

Permutations, setting suns outside the car.   resemblance a
prayer of joy.   it's so meaningless to eat distress and
clarity.   but few invitations found friends away from me
smiling and doing just what I want.   refusing to move.
pregnant audience to all words.   paradoxical integuments.
muscle confronts shadow.   the carelessness of your scissors.
evidence of the sun in the one ecliptic thought.   unturned
you say how these pages are gone into.   the quality never
worth it we pick up whole confederate ice.   an unceasing
image of hope and trouble with possible meanings of beauty.
words want the meaning of my emotions.   resemblance setting
this sense, and this drive to self-knowledge the even rib.
they sip honey, pale, slowly rehoused.   the shadow reaches
the text in a metaphysical landscape.   nothing ever happens.
it remains intact.   find the reader?   Each one of us.

warmth of an intimate day thought between them. where the emotions scale off and intercourse and sleep has a ripped ear. I walked in and found you in bed. the lights flicker on and off in my mind. I can't remember what I read. and so we agreed to place it outside us, an evening deferred, so that it might not constantly interrupt us in the search for its meaning.

A city filled with leisure and softness, it will come into
your body as into a morning world. *I pray that these things
never end: The sand and the sea, the rush of the waters,
the crash of the heavens, the prayer of the heart. The sand
and the sea, the rush of the waters, the crash of the
heavens, the prayer of the heart.* The course of pressures
that should be a definition of the human world, the response
in deference to the echo of biography. I can feel it a block
away. Say total destruction. 'You can have it by being in
it, but in words it is not possible to have it.' Suspenders
knock the other jaw palm-black. We have been speaking to you
since you left us. Now you are entering the world.

Other O Books

Return of the World, Todd Baron, $6.50

A Certain Slant of Sunlight, Ted Berrigan, $9.00

Talking in Tranquility: Interviews with Ted Berrigan, Ted Berrigan, Avenue B and O Books, $10.50

Mob, Abigail Child, $9.50

It Then, Danielle Collobert, $9.00

Candor, Alan Davies, $9.00

Turn Left in Order to Go Right, Norman Fischer, $9.00

Precisely the Point Being Made, Norman Fischer, Chax Press and O Books, $10.00

Time Rations, Benjamin Friedlander, $7.50

byt, William Fuller, $7.50

The Sugar Borders, William Fuller, $9.00

Phantom Anthems, Robert Grenier, $6.50

What I Believe Transpiration/Transpiring   Minnesota, Robert Grenier, $24.00

The Inveterate Life, Jessica Grim, $7.50

A Memory Play, Carla Harryman, $9.50

The Quietist, Fanny Howe, $9.00

Values Chauffeur You, Andrew Levy, $9.00

Dreaming Close By, Rick London, $5.00

Abjections, Rick London, $3.50

Dissuasion Crowds the Slow Worker, Lori Lubeski, $6.50

Catenary Odes, Ted Pearson, $5.00

(where late the sweet) BIRDS SANG, Stephen Ratcliffe, $8.00

Visible Shivers, Tom Raworth, $8.00

Kismet, Pat Reed, $8.00

Cold Heaven, Camille Roy, $9.00

O ONE/AN ANTHOLOGY ed. Leslie Scalapino, $10.50

O TWO/AN ANTHOLOGY: What is the inside, what is outside? What is censoring? What is being censored?, ed. Leslie Scalapino, $10.50

O/3: WAR, ed. Leslie Scalapino, *$4.00*

O/4: Subliminal Time, ed. Leslie Scalapino, $10.50

Crowd and not evening or light, Leslie Scalapino, Sun & Moon and 0 Books, $9.00

The India Book: Essays and Translations, Andrew Schelling, $9.00

A's Dream, Aaron Shurin, $8.00

Picture of The Picture of The Image in The Glass, Craig Watson, $8.00